C000004518

Morning Cloud is Empty

[signature]
23/02/2023

TOLU' A. AKINYEMI

First published in Great Britain as a softback original in 2023

Cover Design: Buzz Designz

Published by 'The Roaring Lion Newcastle'

ISBN: 978-1-913636-38-8
eISBN: 978-1-913636-39-5

THE ROARING LION
NEWCASTLE LTD

Email:
tolu@toluakinyemi.com
author@tolutoludo.com

Website:
www.toluakinyemi.com
www.tolutoludo.com

PREFACE

I'm delighted to publish my fourteenth poetry publication. This is no mean feat, considering that I published my first collection of poems, "Dead Lions Don't Roar," in 2017. The journey has been filled with many literary successes and learning along the way.

Ardent readers and followers of my books know what to expect: books that touch on every facet of the human experience. My latest body of work, "The Morning Cloud is Empty," was birthed from a place of literary lushness. Many of the poems in this collection speak to our collective experiences, and I believe they will resonate with non-readers and lovers of poetry alike.

It's super exciting to have become a walking human library – a god in a human body. Writing across the genres of poetry, children's literature, short stories, and essays has helped to improve my love for the inherent power of words and their ability to transport us to places ordinary eyes cannot fathom.

I sincerely hope that I am able to write more books in the future to cater to new audiences and returning lovers of my work. Being a favourite author to many is deeply satisfying, and I hope my literary journey inspires you.

I hope you enjoy reading this collection of poems as much as I have enjoyed writing it.

'Till next time—don't stop roaring!

DEDICATION

To my Queen, Abigail Akinyemi - I love you
now and always.

ACKNOWLEDGEMENTS

I'm grateful to God Almighty for the wisdom and ability to put pen to paper for yet another time. I do not take my gifts and talents for granted.

A big thank you to my booktiful partner and friend, Olabisi, for the unending support on my literary journey. When the big money comes, I won't forget you. ☺

To my charmazing children, Isaac and Abigail Akinyemi – thanks for your support and for always believing that the **great** 'Lion of Newcastle' is the best poet alive. ☺

Sincere thanks to my wonderful parents, Gabriel and Temidayo Akinyemi, for your endless and immeasurable support of my literary journey.

To my editors, Jen Campbell and Diane Donovan – thank you for being a vital part of this booktiful journey. And to Adeola Gbalajobi, for the initial edits of this collection. Your effort is greatly appreciated.

Thank you to the editors of the following magazine, who gave the following poem its first home. *Hill of Hope* first appeared in Black Moon Magazine.

To everyone who has supported me on my journey to literary acclaim – your support is greatly appreciated.

Contents

Float

I invite you to float through
the immaculate corridors;

swim across four rivers.
We could be forerunners

standing tall like four pillars.
                  Warriors.
Steely men of war eras.

Plunge into broad rivers.
Wade through chaotic disorders.
We could be the foragers of night and turbulent waters.

My Name

My name is an incantation
in my grandmother's mouth,
a deity spitting fire and mysteries.

I am the instrument of war, and she:
                                battle-weary.

She unwraps my origin like delicate china;
appeases my forebears while her tongue
waltzes in obeisance.

God is worthy of our praise - Toluwalope
fated to be a warrior; – Akinyemi,
Crown of Wealth.

My name is fragile art;
a painted heart on canvas.

I am the poem
and Grandmother is a wordsmith
bending me into form.
My name is a prayer
unfolding layers of praise.
My name is a sacrifice of
thanksgiving.

The Morning Cloud is Empty

like my mind:
a diary, empty of emotions.

I am caught in the crossfire of factions.
Love and indifference battle for the land
in my chest.

I am scared of reaching, yet I want closure.

I've become an audience
to the unfolding plot
of my life.

Her Death

took a part of me:
the part that feels.

I've become a relic of something once alive.

Grief clothes my soul in
the grey sky of my heart.

What is this thing about vanishing—
this dark act of dying?

One day she was here; the next
she was a flame travelling
in the wind.

Her death took me apart.

Not the One

They say she is flawed like a
badly sewn dress.

That she is the wrong choice.

They point out her faults like
antiques in a museum. Yet

they just can't see
the memorabilia of scars she carries —

the hurts nestled from all her attempts
to prove them very wrong.

When the Morning Is

Crying:
              growing blisters   masquerading
as red clouds;

In agony
              blistering   waves   disguised
as hailstorms—

When the morning blurts out   the pangs
                                        of evil
springing up   in murky waters,

it's all impregnable.

Pandemic of Empty Pockets I

The pound is losing weight
and our economy is no longer
a prized darling.

The pounds shrink
and our pockets are pounded
like a boxer on the ropes.

We are the ashes of absurd governments.
Policies label us: conservative tools,
The pawns of oligarchs.

Death to benefits.
Death to open borders.

The working classes are labouring.
Mortgage rates are an indignant wind.

The living are counting the cost of surviving
and the pandemic of empty pockets has
placed us in a chokehold.

Hurting

A fairy lady appeared to me
the night I was sex-starved;
seduced me 'till we locked tongues and joined
our bodies
in a dance of pleasure.

I woke up panting
from succumbing to the spirit of deception.

Every now and then, vile demons visit
my habitation to test my spirit-man…

and they pull me down when my wall of defence
looks shaky and I lose   my guard.

Chained to Hopelessness

My best friend was beaten.
A defeated boxer, torn apart
by the one he calls *lover*.

My presence gives him panic attacks.
I tell him he is a paper tiger
trapped in the stripes of love.

My best friend has been crushed
in the rubble of love.

He acts like a tamed lion:
a prisoner of love chained
to a hopeless union

'till death do wrench them apart.

Pretentious

Your pretence is driving her nuts
but she keeps a cool head; stays afloat
amid those raging storms.

This love is a mirage.

Its eggs have long cracked
but you are wrapped in a shawl of deceit.

Soon, emotions will spiral — a river
overrunning its bank.

Falling

I'm falling
in love
with a
woman
I met
last week.

Our hearts
are singing
love blues.

There is
a chemistry,
a longing,
hearts
threatening
to burst
when our
hands touch.

I'm falling
in love
with a
woman
who can
never be
mine,

I'm falling
into a gully

of illusion
and wild,
wild dreams.

Tender Soul

Woman, your soul is tender
but the cruelty of the world has
made you a steaming soup.

Woman, you are petalled.

Woman, you are kind:
so let the stream of love

inside you wash away the bitterness
clinging to your soul.

Guard Your Peace

I have learnt the language of peace, the
sanctuary of solitude.

I no longer give audience
to loud and uncouth men.

There are days I embrace the stillness
of the night, enraptured in the bliss of darkness.

I prize my peace above all else,
for this calming sea is
the anchor of a stable life.

Walking Away

Who joined these strange bedfellows in a union
that should never have been?

Their love language was malice and cold air.

When he walked away, the shackles of the union
were forever broken. But —

the regrets and pain lasted
like a strong scent.

Pandemic of Empty Pockets II

Cut your coat to fit your deflated size.
Cut your coat to the specifics of this pandemic
of empty pockets.

Inflation is a turbulent sea
tipping boats and sinking
$$dreams.$$

Cut your coat to cover your rising bills.
Cut your coat as we trudge on
this poverty hill.

The cost of living is an all-consuming current
and we are far adrift
from the seashore.

Cut your coat before your pockets fill up
with saltwater.

Pandemic of Greed

He was buried on Greed's ground
just like the one before,
which life's damning fate befell
and many others unknown.

He is entangled in a maze of sleaze
in manmade dungeons.

These streams of calamities are
self-inflicted arrows.

These watermarked weaknesses
have become pain points
in our eternal reality.

Leaking Vaults

The vaults of secrets have been opened.
Our Saint has his hands muddied.

Helios has a stagnant pool of a memory.
A bloody hypocrite is playing on the radio.
The bus driver is barking — a bewitched dog:
'Everyone is a hypocrite.'

The vault of secrets is a dung heap,
and banana peels are causing men to slip.

The anti-corruption police are chasing
shadows; chasing the innocent
'till they ignite a revolution.

The vaults of secrets have been blown
                    open,
but we are not learning from what has come before.

Mammy Water

These water bodies harbour strange spirits.
They once swallowed a great fighter
like he was a morsel of pounded yam.

There is a spirit raging beneath the surface,
flustered about fables, and I am
not one to fall for cock-and-bull stories.

The Mediterranean Sea has even more debris—
more than the human mind could fathom,

fathoms below.

Poet of Conscience

I am a poet of conscience,
truth is the cross I bear.
Like Paul on the road to Damascus,
I have submitted my pen
to the government of light.

Pandemic of Greed II

The creed of greed is an anthem
orchestrated on phantoms; on
green shrubs withering in summer months.

These ruinous appetites of Greed's creeds
smoulder fires and shine the light.

Missiles

Our love was toxic.

When our anger raged like a furnace,
Mitchell said *it's fire for fire*, so every day
we fired those bullets, killing happy memories.

Is this the pain of love?
Is this the signal of the end?

Whitewash

Whitewash the devil and clothe him
in messianic robes.

Canonize the evil deeds and wash him clean
at the altar.

Would mercy not speak?
Could compassion not strengthen the weak?
Should kindness not erase everything bleak?

Whitewash the devil
and paint him snow-white.

Pandemic of Empty Stomach

When the stomach is creaking
and the house is an empty shell,
the language of dreams reaches
a menopause.

Mama's anguish sleeping in
sunken eyeballs;
her body language a fiery force.

Hunger breeds
        anger.

        A recipe for danger.

When the stomach is groaning,
these solemn reminders are
self-defeating blows.

Break Bones

We are an amalgamation
of rubble.

Construct our ruins
brick
      by
           brick;

break bones of clay
with iron fists;

melt iron hearts
with candle wax.

Losing the War

We are losing the climate war to
faux
      posturing
           and
                individualism.

Our forests are burning and
                    rains

no longer wet the ground.

We pray, but the clouds are no longer
          gathering.
We can see neither
the ark
               nor the rainbow.

Our planet is set ablaze by
          capitalist emissions:
our greed is swallowing
the green of the earth.

Talking Drum

The baobab is talking to me.
It carries messages like the *agidigbo* drum.
I hear the whispers of spirits;
I hear the wind's sighs.

The baobab is talking to me,
but I no longer commune
with those strange spirits.

The Morning Cloud is Empty II

The morning cloud is empty.
A bird with no feathers is dancing in the sky.
I'm talking to the wind.

The morning cloud has no face.
At the seafront, the ocean is in deep slumber

and the morning cloud watches over it.

The morning cloud is a temple of silence.
I soak in this serenity with reckless surrender.

Vestiges

We are vestiges of the water rising:
tools of warfare.

We are broken songs
swallowed by a multitude of voices.

We sing elegies before sunset:
       for dreams trapped in still bodies;
       for bleeding gardens;
       for those buried in empty clouds.

We are vestiges of a dying world,
memorabilia of hurt,
antique pain,
and everything in-between.

Washed

He was
a mixture of pain and rage
that the soothing words
on the page could not heal.

There was
a turmoil within that
shipwrecked him.

He was
a contraption of hate that
killed our blooming love.

There was
a sea of negativity that
washed him away from our
bloodlines and

severed him from the family tree.

Conveyor Belt

Spirit of the morning,
let your kindness engulf us.
Lift us up.

Spirit of the morning,
dismantle the stumbling blocks
forming a barricade in our way.

Spirit of the morning,
wash away these grim clouds,
these looming droughts,

and bring wildflowers springing
            onto
            our

conveyor belt of goodness.

Stream of Hope

On the tablet of my heart
there is a hummingbird and a dancing tree.
My brain freezes at intervals —
a melting pot of life's worries.

What is life without pain;
without the ache that stings the heart?

I have been pounded by storms
and my mood has been soured
by this evil wind.

But the tablet of my heart
is still filled with hope.

Storms of Death

Arwen, Barra, Corrie, Dudley, Eunice, Franklin, Gladys,
Herman, Imani, Jack, Kim, Logan, Méabh, Nasim,
Olwen, Pól, Ruby, Seán, Tineke, Vergil and Willemien.

What do these names have in common?
These evil winds with deadly fangs.

The storms are eating
the living. Mother Nature's anger is
on a collision course—

Falling trees…
The living have become fallen trees—
souvenirs.

The voice on the radio is a storm of emotions
angry with Mother Nature
and her unforgiving heart.

Hill of Hope

On this hill, we rise
and die.

We elope
from this sinking pit.

On this hill, we rise
and shine.

We provoke
the gods to come to our aid.

The needy are crying to the needy.

We cover our faces in the mud.
My hands bite the dust in my left pocket
and leave a hole in my heart.

On this altar of sacrifice
we are like children in need.
We die on this hill of hope.

Hill of Broken Dreams

We are forgotten towers
devoured on the hill where
dreams gather dust like
moribund trucks.

We are children with suffocating fantasies:

children who die on the hill
where dreams scream
before disappearing into the storm.

Hill of Life and Death

We are children of the rising sun and
the retreating moon.

Encapsulate our lives with the
word 'fleeting.'

We are prisoners in the tapestry of
Life and Death,
Afterlife and Earth.

What is life worth without requiems?

Life transitions into death-
bliss tangles with mourning.

I clutch at the memories of my Nana and
Papa like a child learning to say his first word.

We are the morning dew
settling on dry grounds.
We are the escaping winds gaping
at the ripped window nets.

Why do we fight to rest?
Why do we grieve the dead?
How do we cheat death?

Life wears an emblem — perennial labour —
and Death is the resting place.

Beauty for Ashes

(For Tolulope Adeyemi)

There is an apple in God's eye;
light serenading where darkness
once straddled.

There is a jewel, flawless,
carrying pregnancies
for nations.

Woman, unwrap the treasures
incubating.

Today, a poet becomes an oracle,
giving wings to restless
birds.

Come, like an empty vessel,
to the river of living waters.

Come
            with guilty entanglements
            and worldly affectations.

Come unabashed,

Woman: rise like the dust.
Climb as a fountain rising.

You are the phoenix
and the world is your footstool.

.

Prayer for Clemency

I prayed, this morning, once again
in scorching pain.
I called on God to swallow these floods
that have eroded our sweat and blood.

We are prisoners of erosion and the rain
of anguish captures our emotions.

God of
> tidal waves
> the rainbow and ark
> (and) five loaves and two fishes,

swallow these floods
and eliminate this ache that has left us
on the floor.

Tonight, I'm floating on the seashore,
my eyes piercing the clouds—
waiting on God to dry these floodplains and
accept our sacrifices, overflowing like rainwater.

The Morning Cloud is Empty III

Alpha, Beta, Delta, Gamma, Omicron—
all of them are causing a stir.

We have become pawns in this game
of lockdown.

No one knows
when a new breed will
thrust us into jail, forgotten men.

Tonight, the BBC headline says
Omicron arrived on our shores
unannounced, like the villain
that comes to plunder a land

South Africa has been painted
with the oil of disdain,
an unending soap
that has made its night's sky
a lonely song.

Raging Sea

When the sea rages

it mangles hope

and life becomes a slithering erosion.

Two

I heard two trees talking
in the dawn of morning
leaking secrets in cracked speech.

I saw two dogs barking
in the dead of night, chasing
shadows like bewitched old souls.

I saw two lovers kissing
under the scorching sun
aggravating my misery barometer
beneath the afternoon heat.

Dreams

My dreams are an unfinished novel
with a quantum of characters.

The living frolick with the dead.

There are nights where I'm the protagonist
breaking down high walls with bare fists.

On others, I'm the villain in harm's way.

Before there are unsavoury twists and turns,
I return to the safety of my lover's arms,
snuggled up like the calming sea.

Dancing Fire

On the dusty road
where men crawled in,
hiding under the shadow of darkness

A young man, floating paper on water,
unzips his innocence.

A multitude of voices prick at the chords
of his heart.

Two flabby breasts rest on quaking hands.

A libido is built on quicksand
and a young man dancing with fire.

Noah's Ark

The wind is howling
And hurricanes pummel like a raging bull.

Mother Nature is throwing tantrums.
Water spirits are letting loose the cannons.

Watertight memories have been swept away
by the gust of obliteration.

These sweeping floods
are drinking blood
while we call on God

to send us Noah's ark
to shield us from these relentless attacks.

We wait, and we wait.

Floating Memories

Bite dust,
ye kin of Judas.
Roll back the clock
before drowning in the sea
of amnesia.

We are all particles
in this sea that washes memories.

Pour grime.
Sow strife.

Amplify this vile narrative,
a creation of floating memories.

Soap of Chaos

The political firmament of the Tories
has birthed horror stories,
crumbling storeys.

We are the specimens
in these messy experiments.

And we are the objects in this
unending soap of chaos.

My Name II

Say my name.
Blow horns which ring like thunder,
until your voices grow coarse
like thick grass.

Roar, with ferocious intent.
Bury false allusions, camouflages,
And all that chameleon skin
lest you become a replica.

You are resilient pillars,
unshakeable under this crushing weight.
You are pregnant rivers;
brooks of promise.

Watermark your footprints on the
map of life.
        Let's bridge these gaps
before we disappear with the wind.

Elections I

My father's house echoes.
Home has lost the familiar laughter
that once kept its flame alive.

We are scattered seeds
rooted in new environments
on the trail of survival.

I told father: *elections have consequences.*
Bad leadership sinks lifelong dreams,
scatters seeds into alien lands, and

turns the home into a caricature.

Elections II

Act 1 Scene 1

It's my turn to set your dreams ablaze.
It's our turn for renewed hope.
The *Change* we promised is murky.
You are the billowing smoke
And our words were all smokescreens:
Specimens of no value.

Act 1 Scene 2

Let the North have this power.
Let the Northern bloc vote its own
kin and
kith:
Vote North;
Vote not a stranger to our land!

Act 1 Scene 3

Let the bastions of integrity, competence,
and national renewal prickle
your conscience,
pinch you, and
set fire to your hearts to ignite
the path to equity, fairness, and justice

lest we all perish under the rubble of these
tribal wars.

Count the Stars

I once took a friend to Ghana on vacation.
No virtues were broken or youthful energy
exhausted.

Why did you bring me here? she asked
after a few morose days.

I retorted, *To take a break
and for you to catch your breath.*

As the last words escaped from
the corridors of my mouth.
the atmosphere became frosty
and the days after were winterish nights.

Who brings a friend on holiday to
count the stars in the sky.
to fantasize under the glare of the
evening moon and get lost inside
the pages of books?

Dataset

I have become part of your algorithm
and my data is on sale to the highest bidder.
Mine me like gold and precious metals;
distil me like a fine wine.

I have become another statistic
of your burgeoning bottom line.
Spam me with your incessant notifications.

I have become just a mere number
in your game of infinites.

My Name III

(Abridged Praise Poetry of the Akinyemi Clan of Osi-Ekiti, Ekiti State, Nigeria.)

I'm the son of the man who possesses the baobab
and coconut trees.
My forebears own the Amudu River
with its larger-than-life fishes
whose necks are longer than giraffes.

I am the son of valiant warriors
who lead weaker
men to the farm.

I'm the son
of the sun
which breathes down on harvests
and gives water to roots in splendour.

My forbearers are hardworking farmers
who stand tall to peel harvested yams.

My name is a badge of resilience.

My Pension Fund Was almost Devoured by a Shark

(On the 6th of November 2022, my Stanbic IBTC pension fund was almost eaten by a shark who had accessed and took over my account)

I woke up today and the sun was lukewarm.
The air was as serene as a boneyard.
A shark is playing smart and fast:
My pension fund is on the cusp of evaporating.

And I am here, handling it with serenity.
Maybe I am feeding off the quiet
of the atmosphere.

A poet's rage
Can be found on the page,
     Open
        like an
            unlocked cage —

why would you fleece
this priest; this oracle of words?

Let my words swim better than you ever could.

Twitter Blue

£6.99 monthly for a badge of legitimacy
for Twitter blue.
I'm an illegitimate poet.
I don't give a f**k
about a white (or blue) tick.

£6.99 to sink into Musk's fantasy island—
F**k Twitter
F**k the establishment and their
sour cravings.

I'll use my pounds and pennies to
end world hunger;
not on a party blundering into darkness.

Who needs a badge of verification
to balloon swollen egos?

I am:
        not a parody;
        not a tool for verification.

I won't sink my hard-earned
pennies in the sand and on ~~fake~~ glory-hunting.

Autumn

Autumn is brown, gold, and yellow.
The trees are empty shells
and the leaves have decayed into earth.

The ambience is crystal clear
and though the cold bites from time to time,
we look forward to the spring.

Bloom, Poet

In the plains of Osi-Ekiti,
before the dusty Harmattan wave
swallowed the morning and
turned us into short-sighted children
sweeping dusty grounds with cracked feet,

Who would have known that treasures
were hidden in the wastelands?

In the fringes of Lagos, where the lowly
put fire to dreams
and prophesies
sounded out like heresies,

Who would have thought that flowers could
blossom
even on the rock?

In Wallsend, near Battle Hill,
my battle cry was a prayer altar.
The Northern winds were a fortress
of indomitable spirit.

Let the clouds break forth;
let the morning clouds fill our barns
with the lushness of the earth.
Let the morning wash away our failings.
Like the morning dew, breathe upon us.

Bloom, poet.

Bloom, architect of words.
Blossom into a forest that prompts
others to roar like thunder and intense lightning.

Author's Note

Thank you for the time you have taken to read this book. I hope you enjoyed the poems in it.

If you loved the book and have a minute to spare, I would appreciate a short review on the page or site where you bought it. I greatly appreciate your help in promoting my work. Reviews from readers like you make a huge difference in helping new readers choose a book.

Thank you!
Tolu' A. Akinyemi

Author's Bio

Tolu' A. Akinyemi (also known as Tolutoludo and the Lion of Newcastle) is a multiple award-winning author in the genres of poetry, short stories, children's literature, and essays. His works include Dead Lions Don't Roar (poetry, 2017); Unravel Your Hidden Gems (essays, 2018); Dead Dogs Don't Bark (poetry, 2018); Dead Cats Don't Meow (poetry, 2019); Never Play Games With the Devil (poetry, 2019); Inferno of Silence (short stories, 2020); A Booktiful Love (poetry, 2020); Black ≠ Inferior (poetry, 2021); Never Marry a Writer (poetry, 2021); Everybody Don Kolomental (poetry, 2021); I Wear Self-Confidence Like a Second Skin (children's literature, 2021); I Am Not a Troublemaker (children's literature, 2021); Born in Lockdown (poetry, 2021); A God in a Human Body (poetry, 2022); If You Have To Be Anything, Be Kind (children's literature, 2022); City of Lost Memories, (poetry, 2022); Awaken Your Inner Lion, (essays, 2022); On The Train To Hell, (poetry, 2022); You Need More Than Dreams (poetry, 2023); and The Morning Cloud is Empty (poetry, 2023).

A former headline act at Great Northern Slam, Havering Literary Festival, Crossing The Tyne Festival, and Feltonbury Arts and Music Festival, he also inspires large audiences through spoken word performances and has appeared as a keynote speaker in major forums and events. He facilitates creative writing master classes for many audiences.

His poems have appeared (or are forthcoming) in the 57th issue (Volume 15, No. 1) of the Wilderness House Literary Review; The Writers Cafe Magazine (Issue 18); GN Books;

Lion and Lilac; Agape Review; Continue the Voice; My Woven Poetry; Black Moon Magazine; Calla Press; African Writer Magazine, the Football in Poetry 2nd Anthology; and elsewhere.

His poems have been translated into Greek.

His books are based on a deep reality and often reflect relationships and life, featuring people he has met in his journey as a writer. His books have inspired many people to improve their performances and/or their circumstances. Tolu' has taken his poetry to the stage, performing his written words at many events. Through his writing and these performances, he supports business leaders, other aspiring authors, and people of all ages who are interested in reading and writing. Sales of the books have allowed Tolu' donate to charity, allowing him to make a difference where he feels it's important and showing that he lives by the words he puts to page.

He is a co-founder of Lion and Lilac, a UK-based arts organisation, and sits on the board of many organisations.

Tolu' is a financial crime consultant as well as a Certified Anti-Money Laundering Specialist (CAMS) with extensive experience working with leading investment banks and consultancy firms.
He is a trained economist from Ekiti State University (formerly known as University of Ado-Ekiti (UNAD)).

He sat for his master's degree in Accounting and Financial Management at the University of Hertfordshire, Hatfield, United Kingdom.

Tolu' was a student ambassador at the University of Hertfordshire, Hatfield, representing the university in major forums and engaging with young people during various assignments.

Tolu' Akinyemi was born in Ado-Ekiti, Nigeria and lives in the United Kingdom. Tolu' is an ardent supporter of Chelsea Football Club in London.

You can connect with Tolu' on his various social media accounts:

Instagram: @ToluToludo
Facebook: facebook.com/toluaakinyemi
Twitter: @ToluAkinyemi | @ToluToludo